The jazz piano program was developed by the
Examinations Department of
The Associated Board of the Royal Schools of Music,
lead consultant Dr. Charles Beale.

This publication is not for sale
outside North America.

ISBN 978-0-634-03306-3

7777 W. BLUEMOUND RD. P.O. BOX 13819 MILWAUKEE, WI 53213

IN ASSOCIATION WITH

PUBLISHING

Visit Hal Leonard Online at
www.halleonard.com

Contents

Introduction

Jazz Piano is a comprehensive, graded learning program covering all the necessary building blocks of jazz playing right from the start. The material is written in a clear, concise manner while allowing complete flexibility in the learning process. The structure of Jazz Piano lends itself to taking optional assessments which are part of each level. Whether or not an assessment is taken, or even available, does not prevent anyone from successfully using the highly focused, easy-to-understand instructions in this book.

Here's an overview of each of the five levels:

○ PIECES – 15 pieces in three catagories– blues, standards and contemporary jazz.

○ AURAL TESTS – Developing listening skills which are necessary in successful improvisation.

○ QUICK STUDIES – Learning to improvise on pieces not heard before.

○ SCALES AND ARPEGGIOS – Developing technical proficiency for the purpose of enhancing improvisation.

○ CD – Packaged with every book in the series. All of the pieces in each level are recorded on the CD. In the SCALES AND ARPEGGIOS SECTION, all the scales and arpeggios are recorded with the exception of an occasional right or left-hand part. The AURAL TESTS and QUICK STUDIES recorded examples are indicated by this symbol ⊙ In addition to the above, there are TRIO TAKES and MINUS ONE TRACKS.

With regard to the RELATED LISTENING suggestions, jazz recordings regularly go in and out of print. If the one listed is not available, choose a compilation CD by the same artist on the same label, or buy a related CD by the same musician or band.

JAZZ PIANO FROM SCRATCH is a separate how to book for students and teachers. This book with CD is a resource that expands and supports the jazz concepts and pieces taught in each level. In addition there is specific information pertaining to preparing for optional assessments.

Special Note: The JAZZ PIANO AND JAZZ ENSEMBLE Assessment Program describes in detail the requirements of the assessments, especially those for Scales, Aural Tests and the Quick Study. It also contains the assessment criteria. The Assessment Program is obtainable from The Associated Board of the Royal Schools of Music, 24 Portland Place, London W1B 1LU, UK. <www.abrsm.ac.uk>

BEDFORD SQUARE BLUES
Richard Michael

Medium Swing ♩ = 126 **Cheerful**

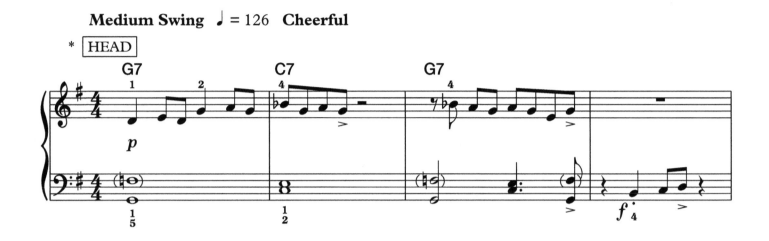

* See Glossary

SOLOS

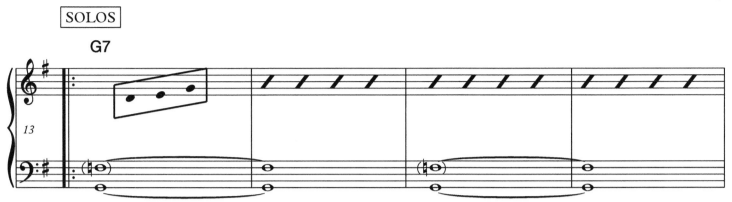

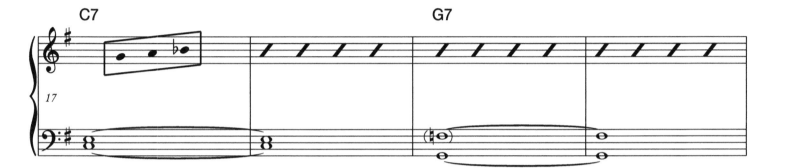

D.C. al Coda
Solo 12 measures in assessment

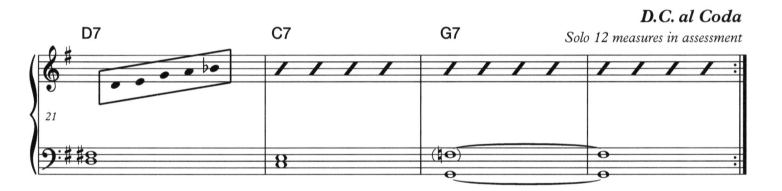

• RELATED LISTENING: Count Basie: "Blues for Joel" from *Kansas City Shout* [Pablo]

O, LORD, PLEASE DON'T LET THEM DROP THAT ATOMIC BOMB ON ME

Charles Mingus arr. Nikki Iles

Slow Swing ♩ = 80 **Lazy**

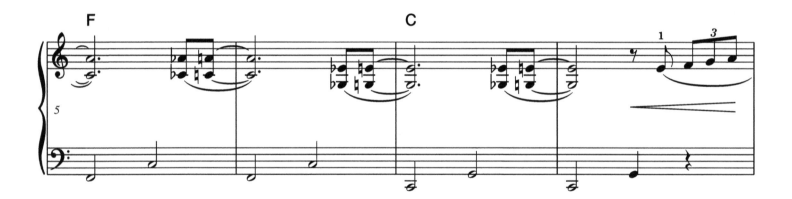

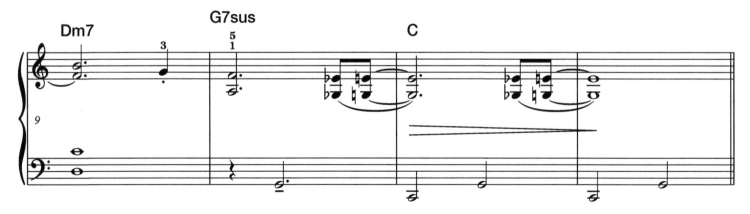

SOLOS

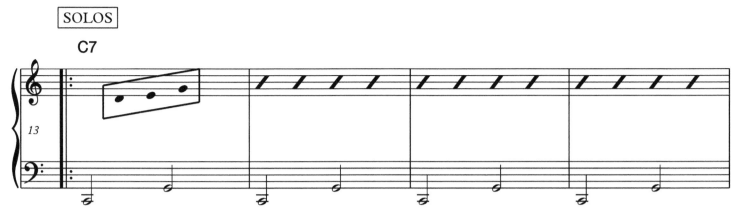

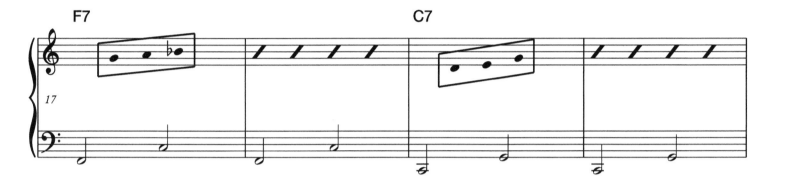

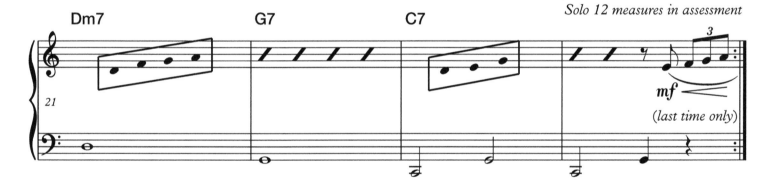

HEAD continues

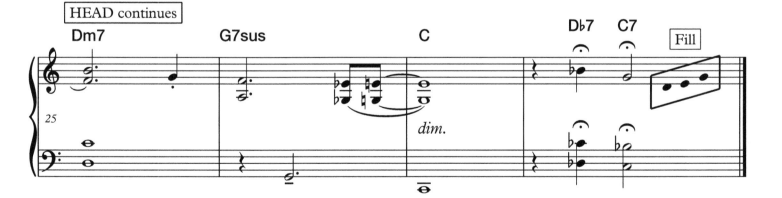

• NOTES: Also try improvising using the major pentatonic on C.

• RELATED LISTENING: Charles Mingus: "O, Lord, Please don't let them drop that Atomic Bomb on me" from *Oh Yeah!* [Atlantic]

*BAGS' GROOVE
Milt Jackson arr. Richard Michael

Medium Swing ♩ = 108 **With a light touch but grooving**

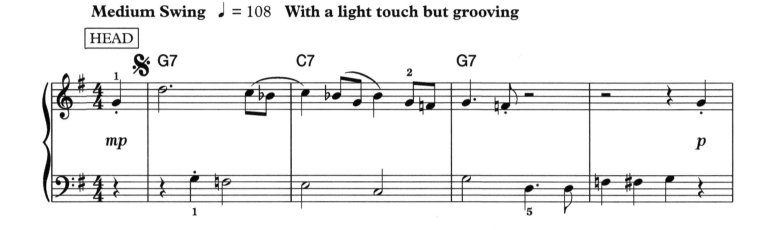

* Minus One – Track 24

SOLOS

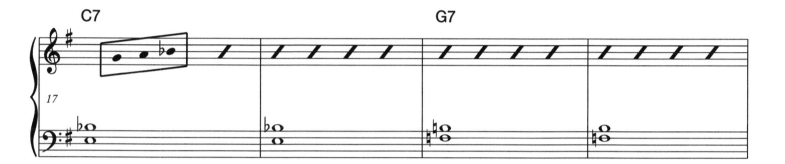

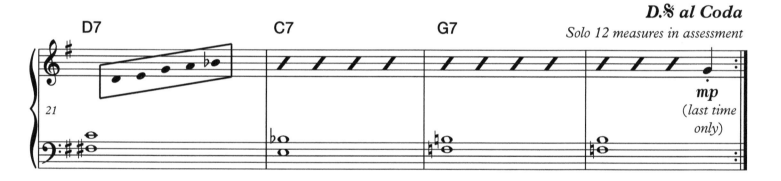

• RELATED LISTENING: The Modern Jazz Quartet: "Bags' Groove" from *Dedicated to Connie* [Atlantic]

SLINKY THING

Simon Whiteside

Slow Swing ♩ = 104 **Slow and slinky**

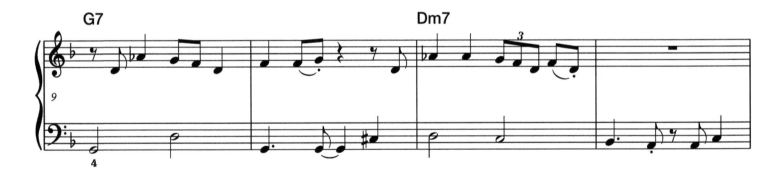

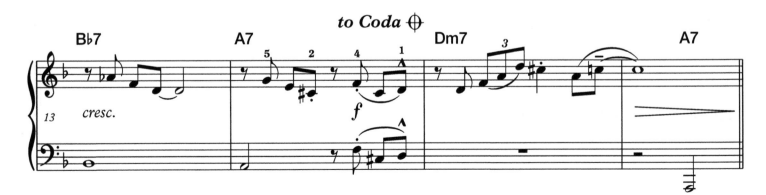

SOLOS

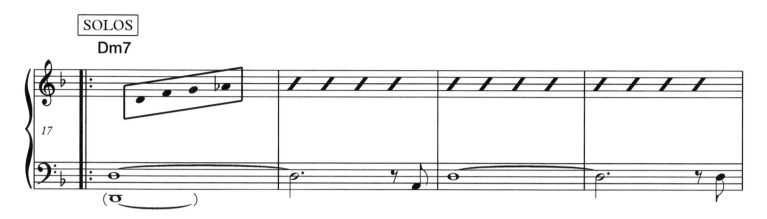

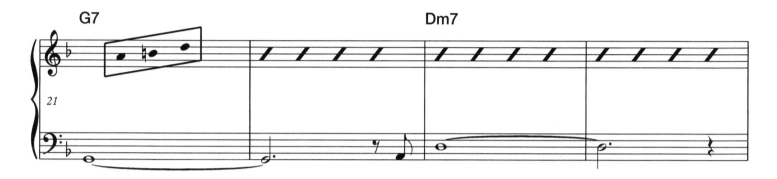

D.𝄋 al Coda

Solo 12 measures in assessment

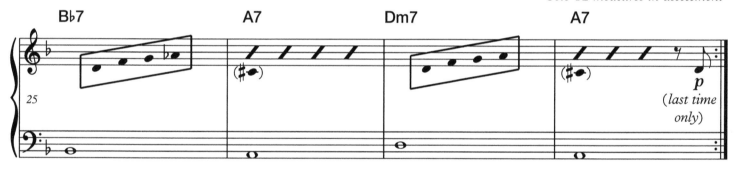

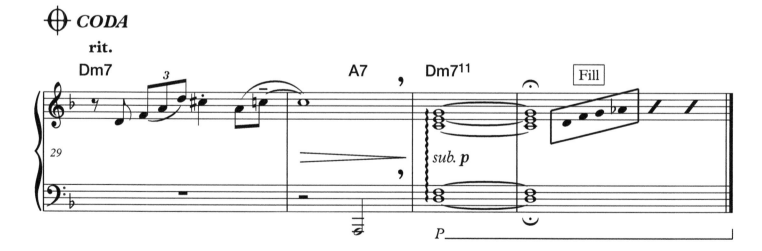

- NOTES: Also try improvising using Dorian on D, and explore using the notes A and A♭.

- RELATED LISTENING: The Nat King Cole Trio: "The Frim Fram Sauce" from *The Best of the Nat King Cole Trio* [Capitol]

PROVE YOU GROOVE
Phil Peskett

Straight 8s Rock ♩ = 108 **Solid, insistent**

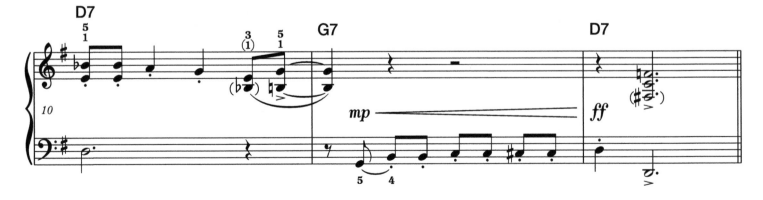

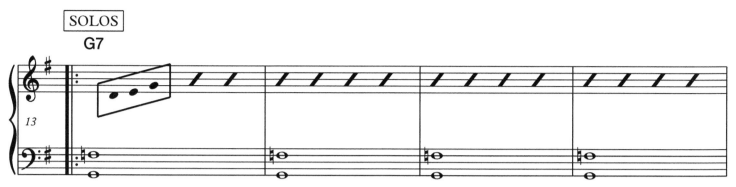

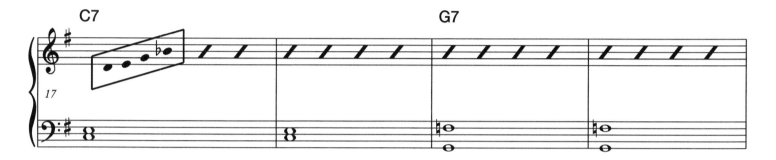

D.C. al Coda

Solo 12 measures in assessment

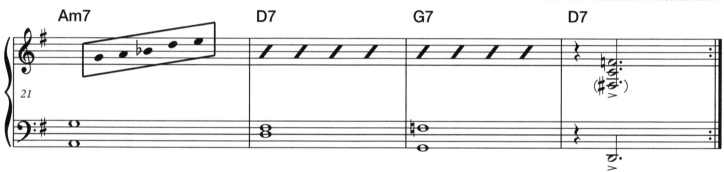

• NOTES: Also try playing the opening left-hand pattern in your solo, e.g.

in the G7 measures and

in measures 17 and 18.

• RELATED LISTENING: Herbie Hancock: "Watermelon Man" from *Takin' Off'* [Blue Note]

*PERDIDO
Juan Tizol   arr. Richard Michael

Medium Swing ♩ = 104   **Grooving**

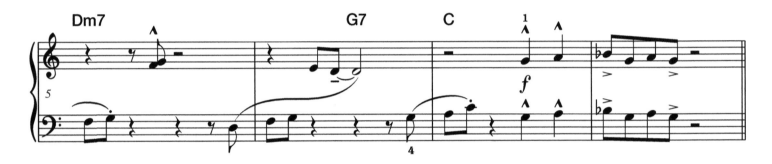

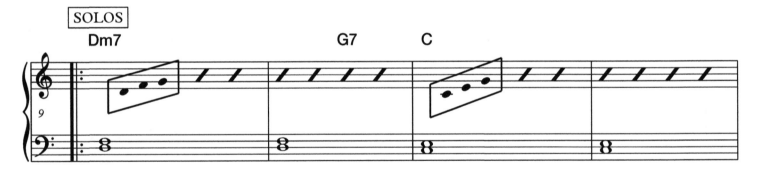

Solo 7 measures in assessment

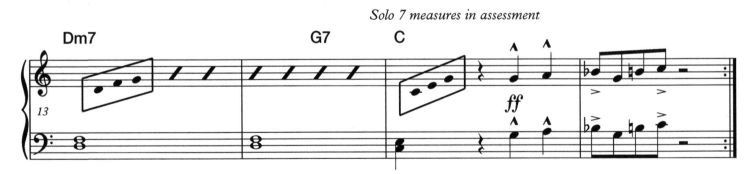

* Minus One – Track 25

HEAD continues

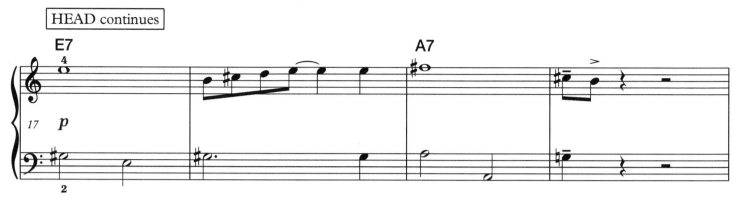

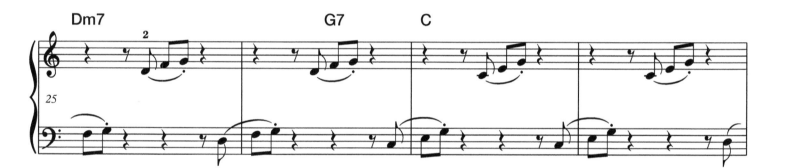

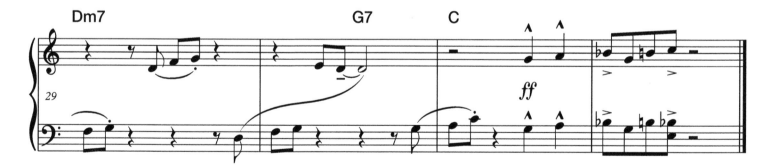

• NOTES: Also try playing some left-hand vamps in your solo, e.g.

in measures 9-10.

• RELATED LISTENING: Duke Ellington: "Perdido" from *In a Mellotone* [RCA]

INCHWORM
Frank Loesser   arr. Nikki Iles

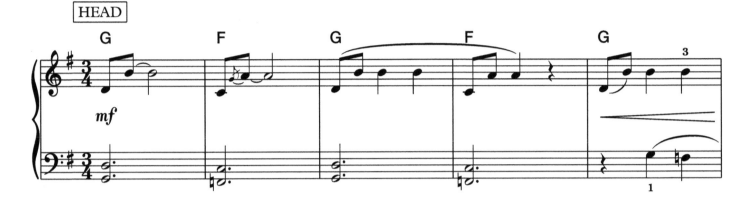

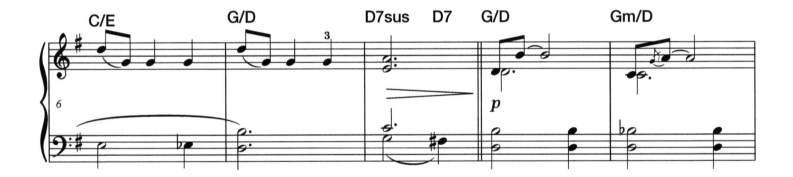

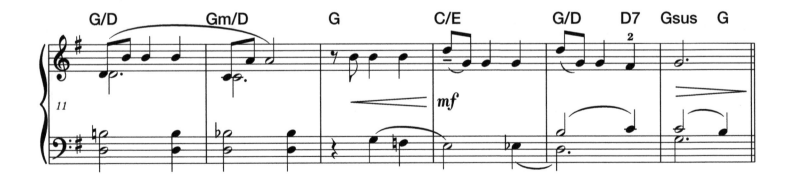

SOLOS

Solo 8 measures in assessment

HEAD continues

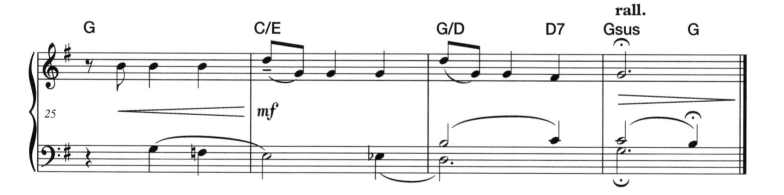

• RELATED LISTENING: Rachelle Ferrell: "Inchworm" from *First Instrument* [Blue Note]

JEAN PIERRE
Miles Davis   arr. Charles Beale

Straight 8s   ♩ = 84   **Slow funk – quiet, insistent**

SOLOS

Solo 8 measures in assessment

HEAD continues

• NOTES: Explore using the notes E and E♭ in your solo.

• RELATED LISTENING: Miles Davis: "Jean Pierre" from *We Want Miles* [Columbia]

(OLD MAN FROM) THE OLD COUNTRY

Nat Adderley & Curtis R. Lewis   arr. Phil Peskett

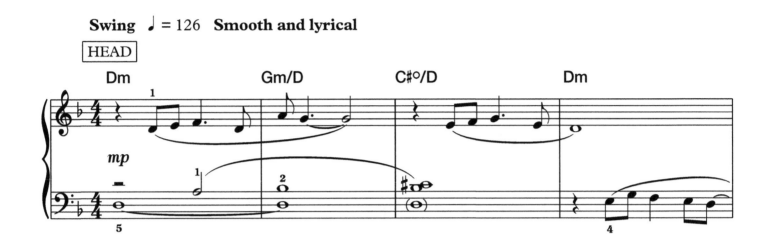

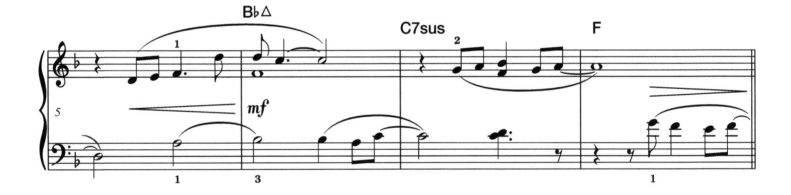

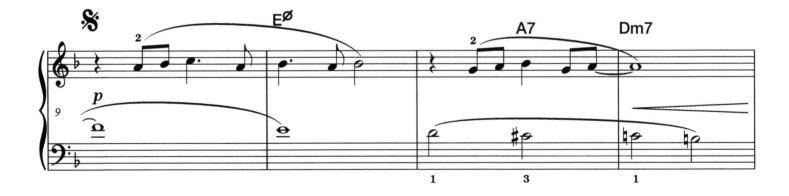

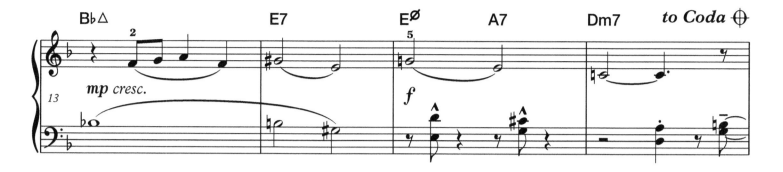

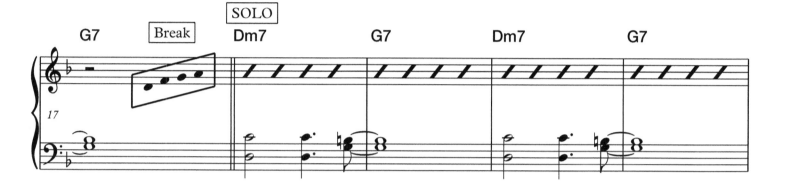

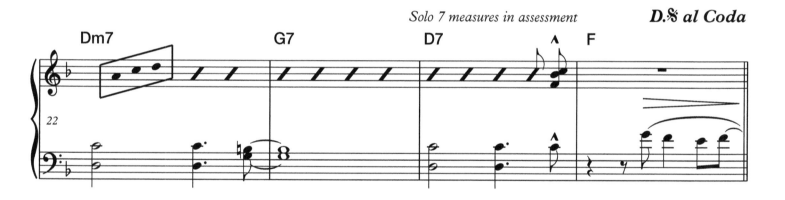

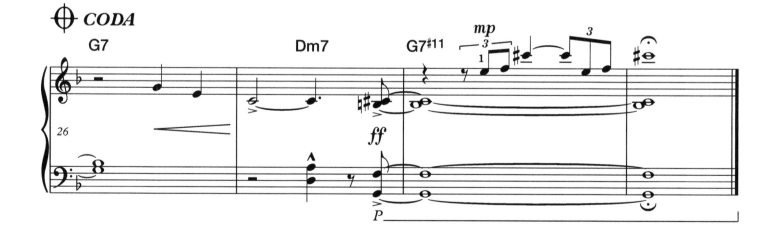

IS YOU IS, OR IS YOU AIN'T (MA' BABY)

Billy Austin & Louis Jordan   arr. Eddie Harvey

Medium Swing ♩ = 152 **Bright**

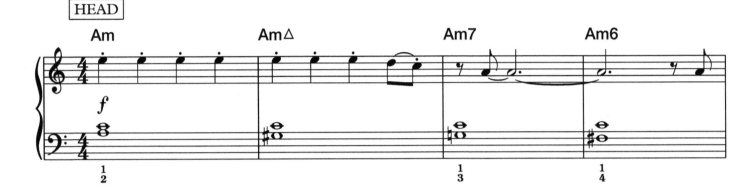

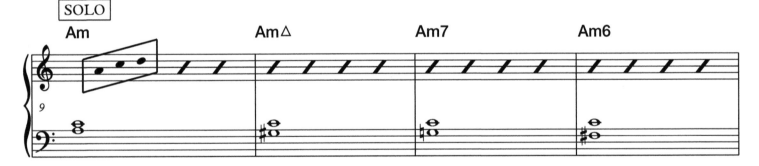

Solo 8 measures in assessment

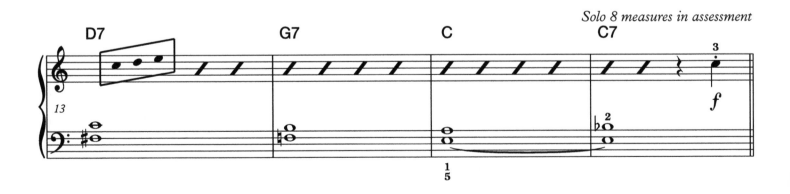

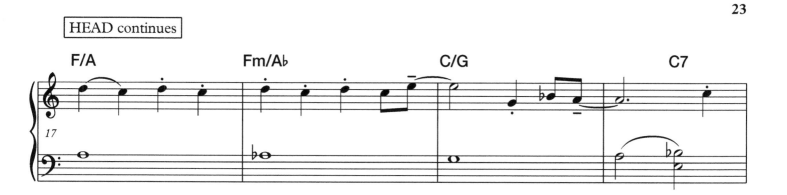

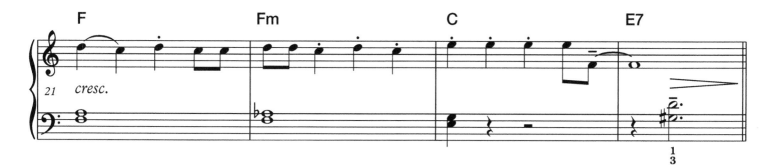

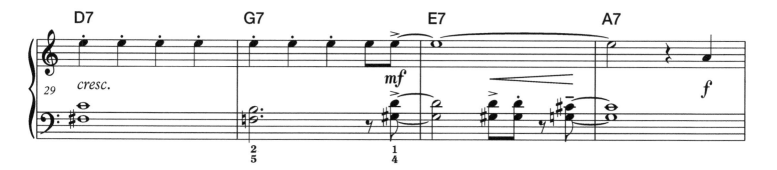

• RELATED LISTENING: The Nat King Cole Trio: "Is you is, or Is you ain't (ma' Baby)" from *Too Marvellous for Words* [Charly]

BOTTLE JUNCTION
Nikki Iles

Medium up Swing ♩ = 108 **Playful**

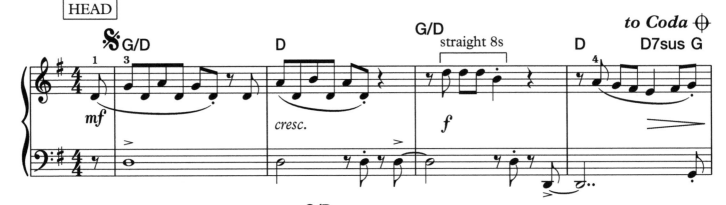

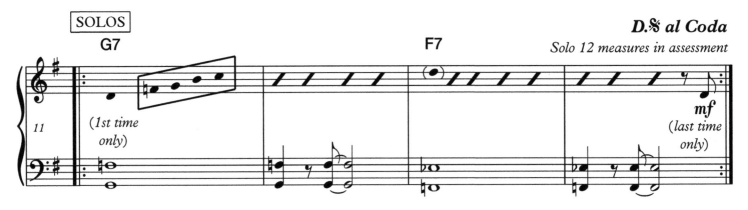

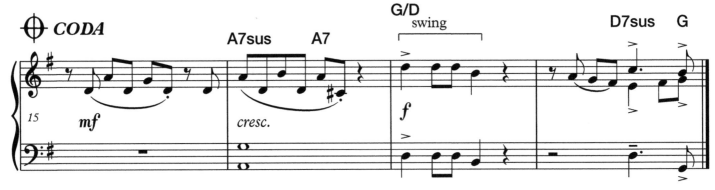

- **RELATED LISTENING:** Paul Bley: *Footloose* [Savoy]

BLUE AUTUMN
Eddie Harvey

HE IS SADLY MELTING
Phil Peskett

Straight 8s ♩ = 66 **With resignation**

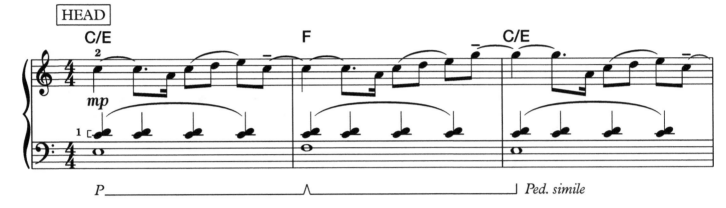

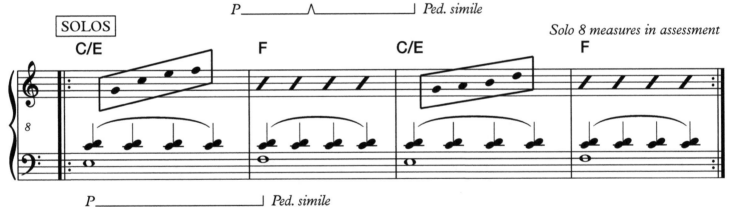

• RELATED LISTENING: Bill Frisell: "Have a Little Faith" from *Have a Little Faith* [Elektra Nonesuch]

HERE WE GO AGAIN
Michael Garrick

Swing ♩ = 104 **Thoughtful**

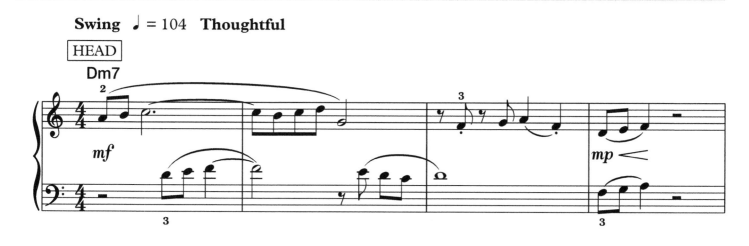

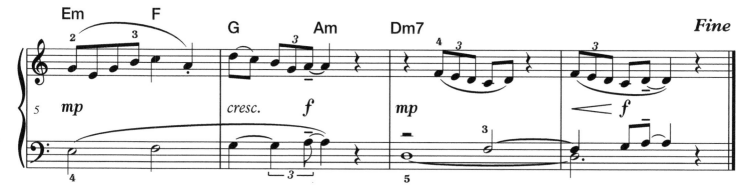

D.C. al Fine

Solo 8 measures in assessment

- RELATED LISTENING: Michael Garrick Trio: "Song of the Elms" from *Parting is Such* [JAZA]

*YOKATE
Huw Warren

Straight 8s ♩ = 132 **Steady African groove**

* Minus One – Track 26

Solo 8 measures in assessment

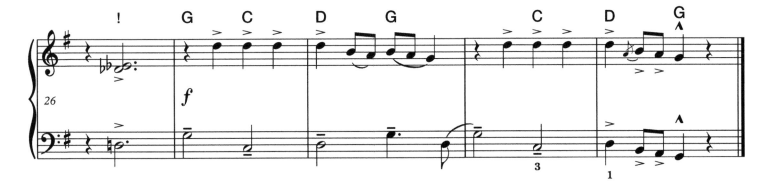

• RELATED LISTENING: Abdullah Ibrahim: "African Sun" from *African Sun* [KAZ]

Aural Tests

Aural and musicianship skills are a fundamental part of jazz performance and improvisation. In solo work jazz musicians must hear in their head the rhythmic and harmonic context in which they are working, in order to respond inventively and stylistically to that sound in their improvisation. In ensemble playing musicians must make choices about their role within the overall texture and the notes or rhythms that are most appropriate to play in the light of what they hear. The aural tests are designed to help you to listen to music in this way and to foster working by ear, the best and often the only way to learn jazz. The best approach is to get someone else to play them for you.

The practice tests

The practice tests can also be extended into fun exercises for developing improvisation and other jazz skills. Preparation for the tests involves doing the same activities as learning new pieces or practising the improvised sections, and you should therefore see them as a natural and familiar part of your learning experience. Questions along the lines of "What feel is this in?", "How many beats in a measure are there?", "How does this rhythm go?", "What's the tune?" and "Can you clap the pulse?" are almost bound to occur in the course of learning pieces and developing improvisation skills.

The chapter on the aural tests in JAZZ PIANO FROM SCRATCH suggests several activities for the development of these vital skills as well as information about the optional assessment. The CD included with this book illustrates how each element of the aural tests will be presented in the assessment and records several of the A Tests. Each recorded test is indicated by the (CD) symbol.

○ TEST A – (A1) Clapping the pulse, (A2) Clapping on a specified beat of the measure, (A3) Clapping the rhythm of a short extract

○ TEST B – Singing as an echo

○ TEST C – Question and answer/improvised answering phrases

Jazz musicians use their aural and analytical skills to fix a clear and detailed inner aural image, or "internal map", of a piece of music in their heads. This map will provide the structure – important rhythmic, melodic, harmonic and formal features – upon which any successful improvisation will be made.

Developing and working on your aural skills is something that you will continue to do for the rest of your life as a jazz musician. It is a fundamental and hugely satisfying part of jazz.

Test A

A1 To clap the pulse of a passage of music in 3 or 4 time played by the examiner. The examiner will commence playing the passage, and the candidate will be expected to join in as soon as possible by clapping the beat.

A2 To clap on the last beat of each measure while the above passage is played again. The examiner will first state the time and count in the candidate.

A3 To clap the rhythm of a short, single-line extract (marked 'X') which will be played twice by the examiner.

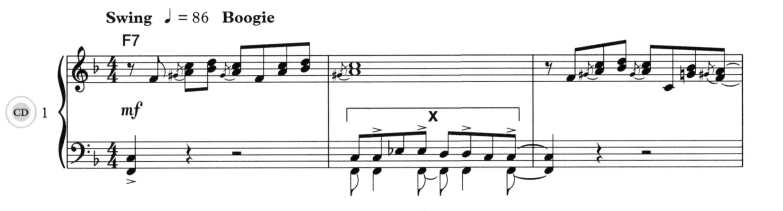

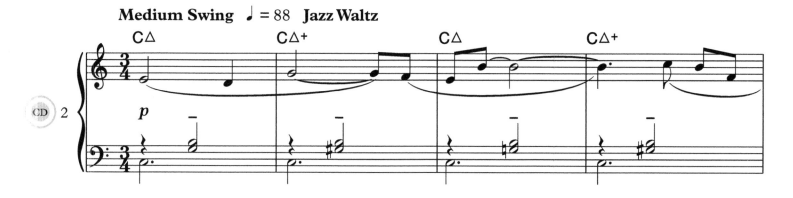

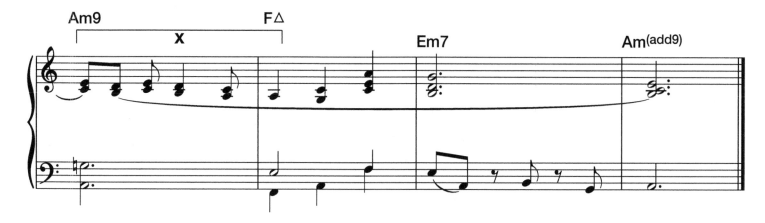

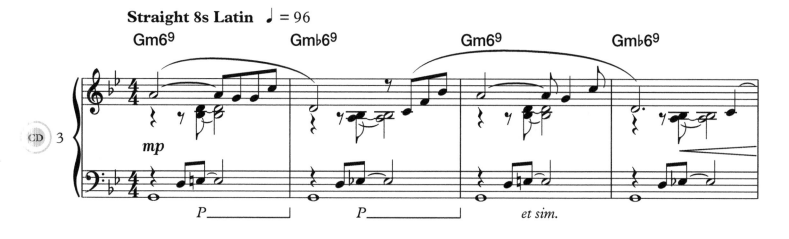

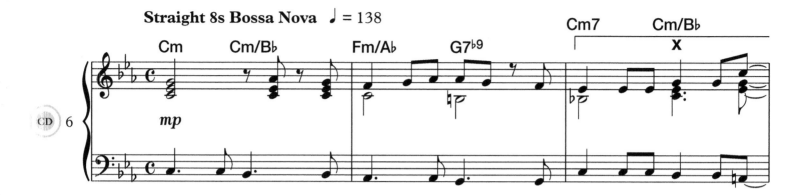

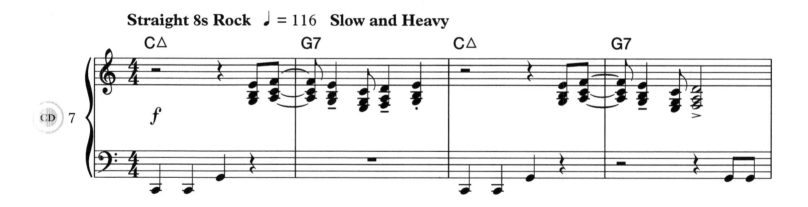

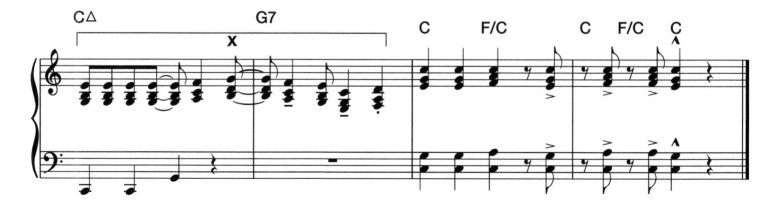

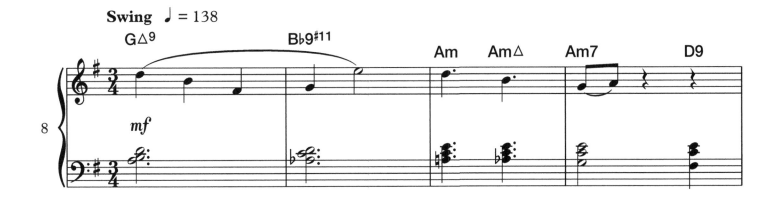

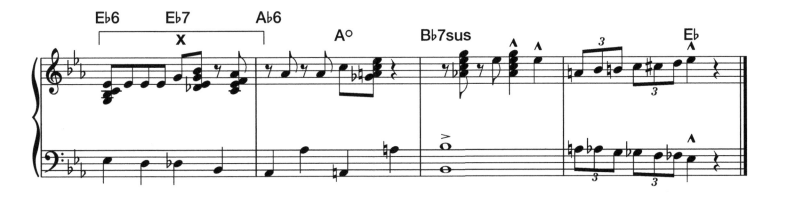

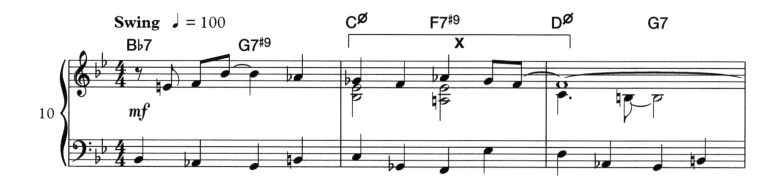

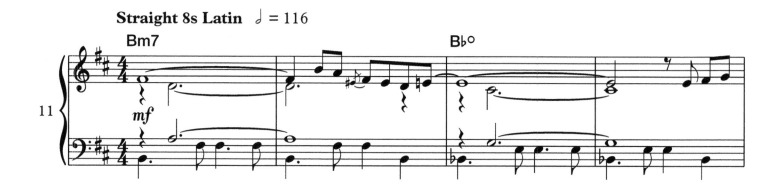

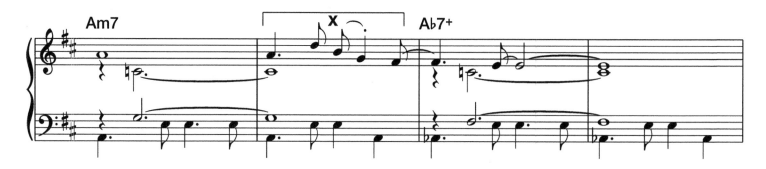

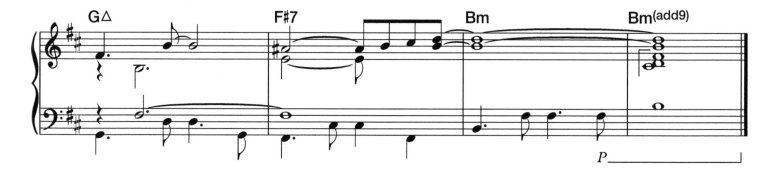

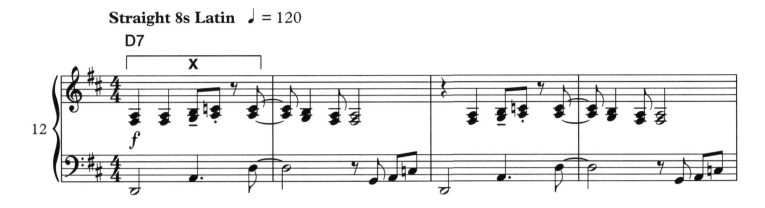

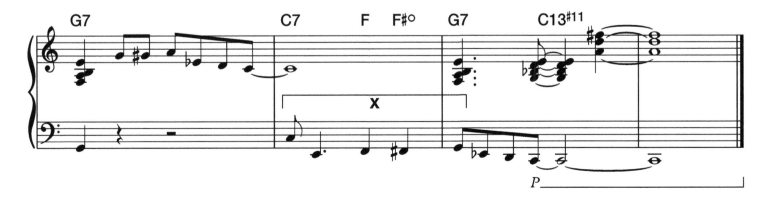

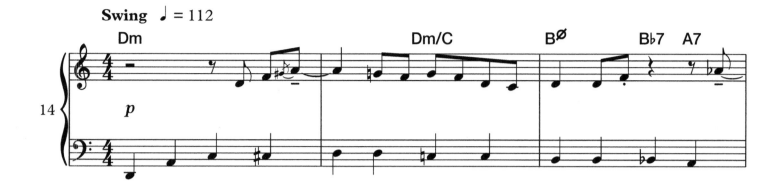

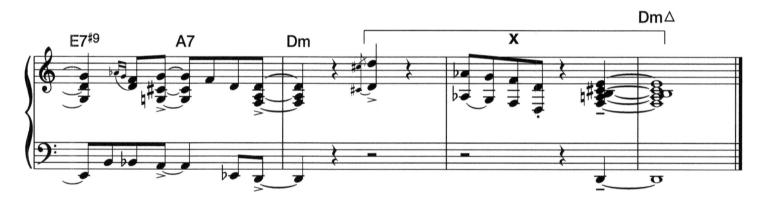

Test B

To sing, as an echo, four two-measure phrases limited to a range of a third in a major or minor key or mode played by the examiner. The echoes should follow each phrase in strict time without an intervening pause. The key-chord, or chord on the root, and the starting note will first be sounded and a two-measure count-in given.

40

Swing ♩ = 120

Swing ♩ = 92 **Jazz Waltz**

Straight 8s Bossa ♩ = 104

Swing ♩ = 132 **Jazz Waltz**

Straight 8s Latin ♩ = 100

Test C

To sing or play improvised answering phrases to four two-measure phrases limited to a range of a fourth (though the answers need not be similarly limited) in a major or minor key or mode played by the examiner. The answers should follow each phrase in strict time without an intervening pause. The key-chord or chord on the root will first be named and sounded, and the pulse given. The examiner will then play four measures introductory groove, before playing the first phrase to which the candidate should respond, and continue with an accompanying groove throughout the test. Your response will have to be played up an octave. If you choose to play this test in the assessment you will be able to use a scale that has appeared in the assessment program by your level. Some of the specimen tests have been written specifically for the singing option and use scales outside of the assessment program requirements.

Straight 8s Latin ♩ = 108

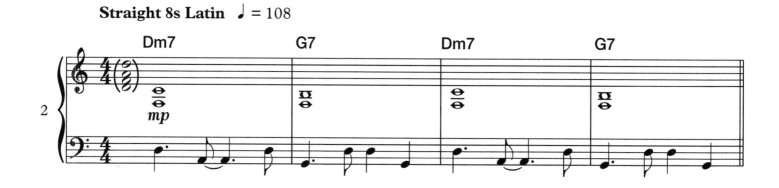

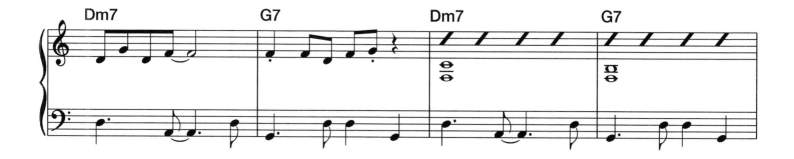

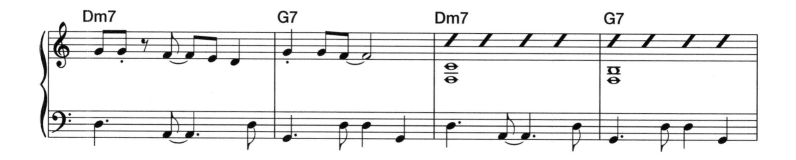

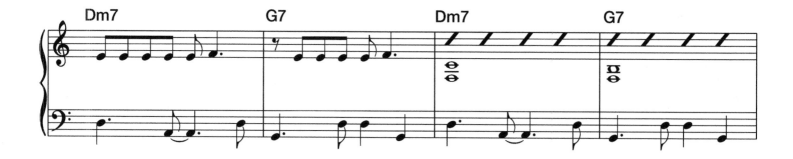

Last time

Straight 8s Rock ♩ = 96

Last time

Swing ♩ = 92

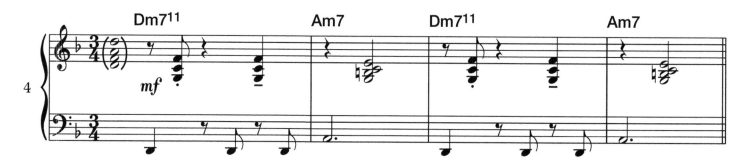

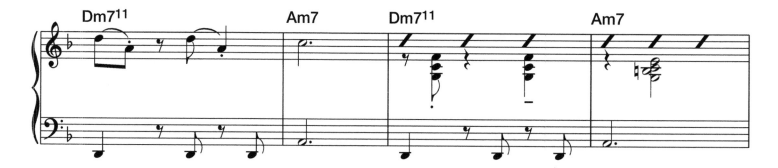

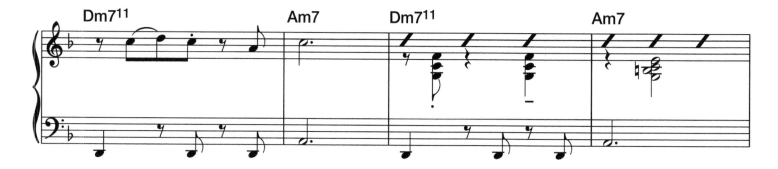

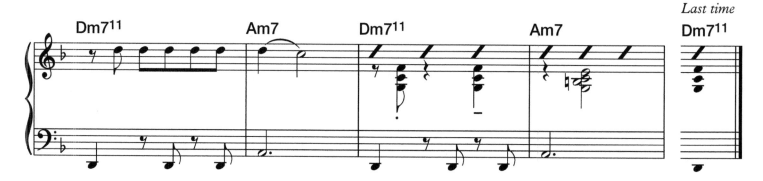

These extra grooves provide further practice for Test C. Get your teacher or friend to invent two-measure right-hand questions over them and improvise your own two-measure answers.

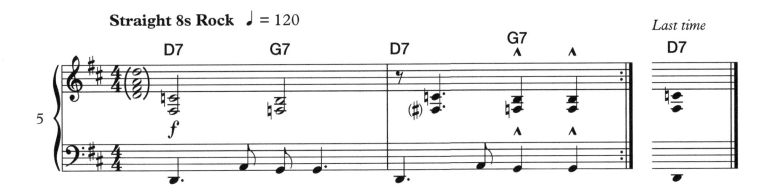

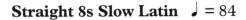

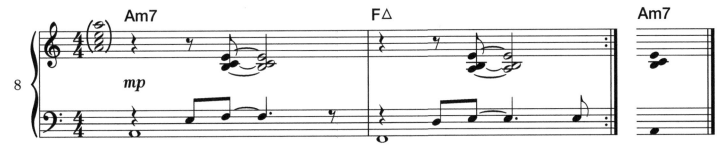

Quick Studies

Playing unprepared in a lively, creative, musical and accurate way is at the very heart of jazz playing. All musicians have their own vocabulary which they use as a basis for their playing; but they must also be able to improvise spontaneously, or "unprepared", on a piece previously unheard. The quick study tests help you prepare for the real demands of unrehearsed situations which are so often a feature of the jazz musician's life.

Jazz is an aural tradition, and the ability to pick up new material and recreate it by ear as well as from notation is vital. Some of the most interesting repertoire cannot be written down satisfactorily, and listening and copying is often the only way to get inside the style of the music, its phrasing, its inflections and its expressive embellishments. Reading staff notation is therefore just one of several ways in which you can learn jazz repertoire; recordings, friends and teachers are other important sources, and the option of doing the quick study by ear is also available. Ask another musician to test you.

In order to learn and really understand the style and the repertoire of jazz from the inside, jazz musicians should regularly practise both reading music fluently and musically from the page and copying music fluently and musically directly from what they hear.

The practice tests

○ GROOVES – The practice tests cover a wide range of musical styles within the idiom. You will play in both swing and straight eighth notes and use swing, rock and Latin grooves. The tempo, indicated by a metronome mark, should also be followed.

○ THE SCALE OR MODE AND GUIDELINE PITCHES – You will be given the scale or mode of the test before playing and, although other pitches may be incorporated as desired, this should form the basis of your improvisation. As in the pieces, guideline pitches are given for those reading from the page, while the name of the relevant scale or mode is given and the initial pitch sounded and named for those working by ear. It is expected that you will be able to use the pitches more flexibly as you progress, working from small three or four-note pitch groups to full scales as fluency and control develop. As a starting-point you might find it useful to try using the same pitches as those in the short head for your improvisation.

○ KEY SIGNATURES – At Level 1 the key signature of the quick study follows that of the scale given on which to improvise.

Ideally you should practise doing the quick studies both ways – by ear *and* from notation – as both are essential jazz skills. Ultimately, however, a successful performance of the quick study depends on the accurate rendition of the head and a suitable and musical improvisation, not on whether you did it by ear or notation.

The CD illustrates how the quick study will be taken in the optional assessment by both "by ear" and "from notation" candidates. Each recorded test is indicated by the symbol (CD) in this book. For additional information about the assessment, see JAZZ PIANO FROM SCRATCH or the ABRSM ASSESSMENT PROGRAM.

To play *either* at sight *or* by ear, at the choice of the candidate, a two-measure passage for one hand only and improvise a two-measure continuation based on the scale indicated and used for measures 1 and 2. This scale will be any one of those set for this Level. The first two measures will be fully notated in 4/4 time and written in the treble clef within the range of a fourth. Chord symbols will also be provided.

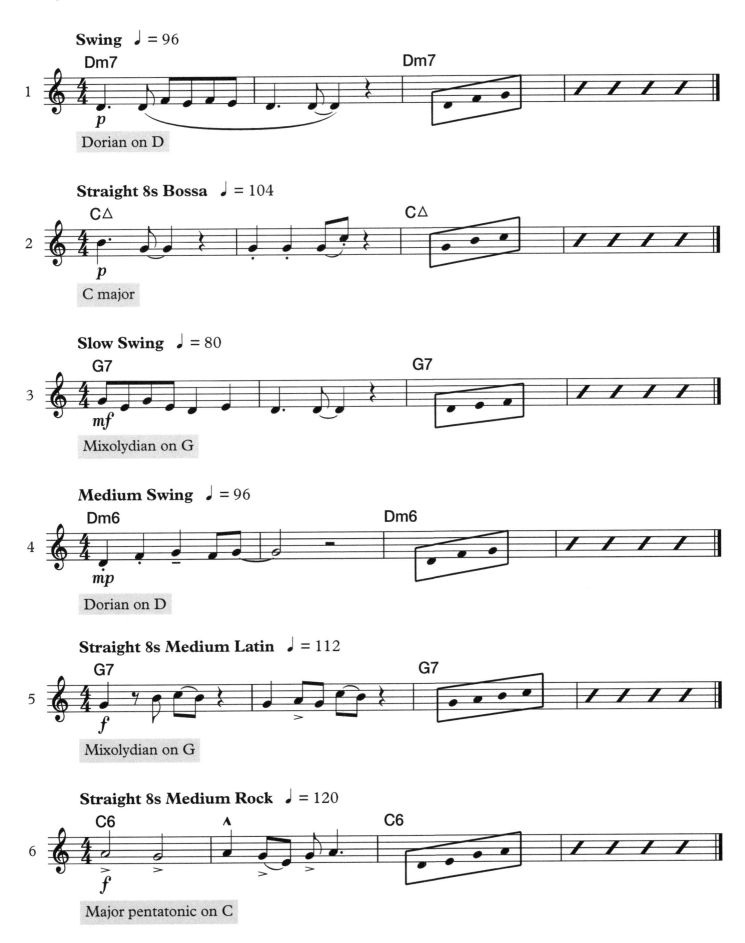

48

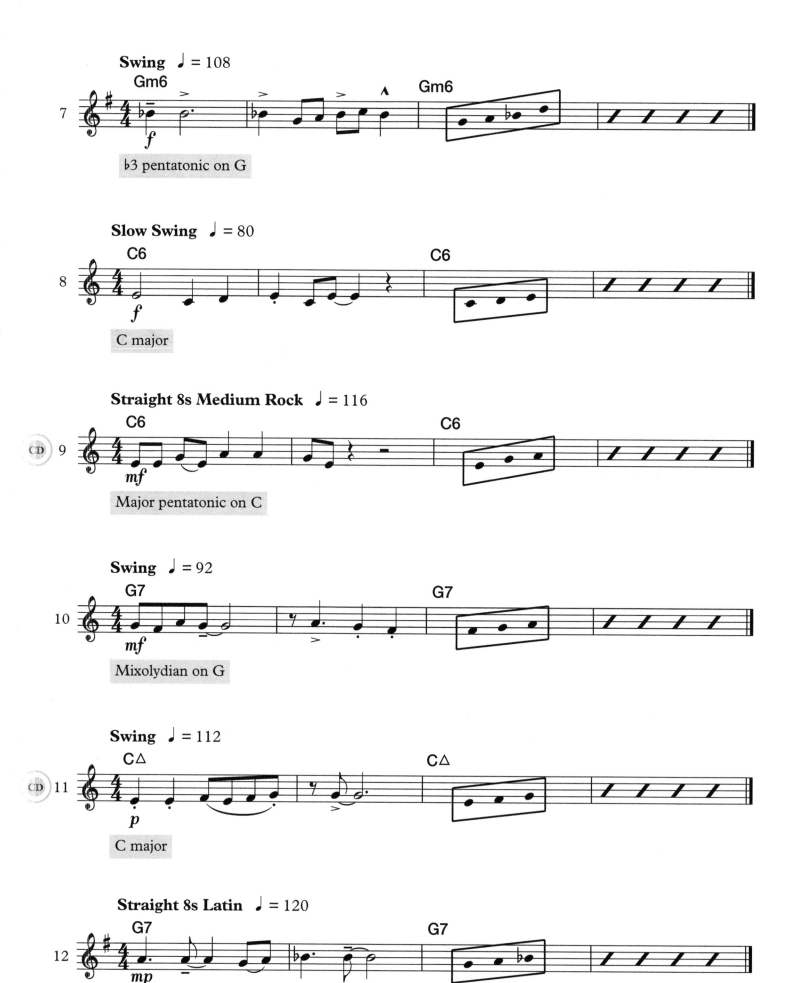

Scales and Arpeggios

All good jazz sounds effortless, but that sense of ease is usually achieved through regular hard work and the skills developed by the practice of scales and arpeggios. The scales in this book have been organized progressively to develop the technical control, flexibility and knowledge of the geography of the keyboard (i.e. where the sharps and flats are) needed in improvised performance. They'll also familiarize you in a systematic way with the common patterns, roots and key centers found in jazz. You'll play patterns like pentatonic and blues scales and various modes, and over the levels you'll build up a variety of these patterns on common roots, like C, F and G. You'll also find that at different levels different keys are emphasized: at Level 1, for example, C major pentatonic on C, Mixolydian on G and Dorian on D are all related to the key center of C. Working through this structure systematically will help you broaden the musical choices you can make as you improvise.

○ FINGERING – The fingerings given are not obligatory; many of these patterns can be fingered in any number of ways. Remember, though, that poor and inconsistent fingering often leads to a second-rate musical result. At the same time, the fingerings have been carefully chosen to prepare you for the most common chord sequences and melodic phrases. In a number of cases alternate fingerings are provided; if you learn these different fingerings, you'll find in performance that you can choose the one which suits the improvisation context best.

○ PRACTICE ROUTINES – There are many ways to practice scales and up to this point they should instead be practised more as they would be used in performance of a piece. In short, be flexible when practising. For example, start on different notes of the scale, change direction at random, use a variety of rhythms, including swing and straight feels and experiment with different shapes, dynamics and articulation. You are also strongly advised to integrate improvisation with scale practice improvising wherever possible. The chapter on scales in JAZZ PIANO FROM SCRATCH provides helpful information on different musical ways to practice scales and the requirements for taking the optional assessment.

The recommended minimum speed for playing scales at Level 1 is ♩ = 60, for playing arpeggios and broken chords ♩ = 46.

Finally, the discipline of practising scales and arpeggios leads to freer, more expressive playing. In the end it really *is* worth the time and effort.

Scales
with each hand separately, straight or swing

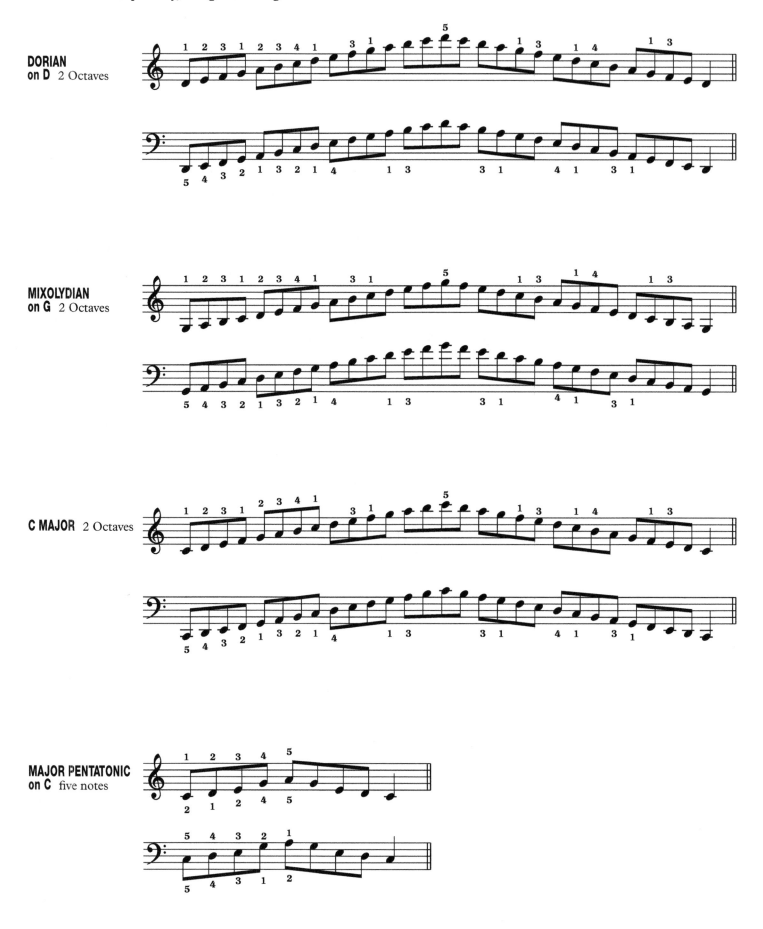

♭3 PENTATONIC
on G five notes

Arpeggios
with each hand separately, straight or swing

G MAJOR 1 Octave

D MINOR 1 Octave

Glossary

anticipation   anticipating a beat by playing a note or chord on the previous eighth note or quarter note

augmentation   process in which the rhythmic values of notes in a phrase are doubled

augmented   altering an interval by raising it a semitone; most commonly, the augmented 4th, e.g. C–F♯

backbeat   the stress on beats 2 and 4 in jazz and rock grooves

beat   refers to a given place in the measure, e.g. beat 1, beat 2, etc. Also used in the context "got a good beat" to refer generally to the style, driving quality and success of a given groove.

bebop   challenging, complex and exciting virtuoso jazz style of the 1940s. Charlie Parker (alto sax), Dizzy Gillespie (trumpet), Thelonious Monk (piano) and Bud Powell (piano) are key names.

boogie-woogie   early 1900s piano style, combining a driving "train-style" left hand with characteristics of the blues. Key players include Clarence Pinetop Smith, Meade Lux Lewis and Pete Johnson.

bossa nova   popular early 1960s Latin jazz style blending Brazilian rhythms and grooves with cool jazz. Key players include Joao Gilberto, Stan Getz, Charlie Byrd and Oscar Peterson. Key composer: Antonio Carlos Jobim.

break   short melodic phrase which punctuates the music, usually while the accompaniment stops

bridge   name for the contrasted B section of a 32-measure standard (AABA), also called the middle eight. May occur in other tunes with contrasting middle sections.

calypso   style of music, dance and song originating in the West Indies, popularized in the 1930s and 1940s, and taken up by jazz musicians including Sonny Rollins, Nat "King" Cole and Dizzy Gillespie. Sometimes characterized by regular accents on beat 1 and the "and" of 2.

changes   name given to the string of chords used in a piece or section of it; "Rhythm Changes" describes the sequence of chords from the bridge of Gershwin's "I Got Rhythm", used in many standards

chord   sound formed by two or more notes played together

chord sequence   led from the bass-line, a series of chords in a repeating sequence that make up the harmonic background to a tune or solo section

chord symbol   concise designation of the notes of a chord placed above the stave (sometimes between the staves), consisting of the root note and a symbol indicating the remaining possible notes, e.g. C△ = a major 7 chord on C, i.e. the notes C E G B. Some chords may be referred to by more than one symbol, e.g. Cmaj7 = C△; D– = Dm. See also triad over bass note.

clave   set of stresses across a 4/4 measure in Latin grooves; pronounced "clah-vay"

closed position   type of voicing in which the notes of the chord are close together

comping   short for "accompaniment". Creation of a rhythmic and harmonic background for your own melodies or for other players' solos.

consonant   description of an interval, chord or general character of a piece or section where the sound is smooth and rounded

degree   name for the pitch of a scale, defined by its position from the root; e.g. the 3rd degree of C major is the note E

diminished   altering an interval by lowering it a semitone; most commonly, the diminished 5th, e.g. D–A♭

diminution   process in which the rhythmic values of notes in a phrase are halved

dissonant   description of an interval, chord or general character of a piece or section where the sound is harsh or discordant

Dixieland jazz   see New Orleans jazz

downbeat   the downbeats are beats 1, 2, 3 and 4, while the upbeats are the "ands" of each of these beats, that is to say the "offbeat" eighth notes, in classical terms. Originally called down and up because of the relationship with dance and the position of the body as down or up.

extensions   notes added to a chord for extra dissonance and richness; named using numbers above 8, most frequently the 9th, 11th and 13th. May sometimes be sharpened or flattened.

feel the way the beat is subdivided. Subdivision into 2 is known as straight 8s; subdivision into 3 as swing.

free jazz The avant-garde jazz of the late 1950s and 1960s, characterized by experiments with atonal and other harmony, using more than one pulse or none at all and a general concern with extremes and breaking the boundaries of jazz. Key players include Ornette Coleman, late John Coltrane and Cecil Taylor.

funky funk was a style of mid-1960s and later American popular music which developed from Motown and Soul, often characterized by repeating sixteenth note syncopations around a 4/4 rock groove

groove name given to the rhythmic character of a piece of music; defined by its bass-line, pattern of accents and offbeats and style. Broad categories are swing, Latin and rock. In jazz, grooves may be varied, particularly in solo sections.

guide tones notes of a chord, typically the 3rd and 7th, which "guide" the harmony by the way they move, creating and releasing harmonic tension

hammering on blues technique describing the addition of a repeated note above a melody, "hammering" with it in the same rhythm

head jazz musician's term for the tune, the often written-out music that comes at the beginning or "top". A common signal at the end of an improvisation is for the leader to point to his or her head, which means "Back to the top, let's play the tune again, I'm finishing my solo."

inner lines contrapuntal lines linking the guide tones in chordal progressions

internal clock a clear sense of the pulse which you feel within yourself

interval the gap between two notes, e.g. minor 3rd, major 7th. Can describe notes played melodically or harmonically.

inversion description of chords, dependent on their bass note. A C major chord with C in the bass is in root position; with E as the lowest note it's in first inversion, and with G in the bass it's in second inversion.

jazz-rock late 1960s and early 1970s style, incorporating jazz improvisation with rock grooves and often electric instruments. Sometimes known as "fusion". Key players include Miles Davis (*Bitches Brew*), Herbie

Hancock (*Headhunters*), the band Weather Report (*Heavy Weather*) and the band Blood, Sweat and Tears.

jazz waltz 3/4 swing groove, often using the characteristic hi-hat pattern

and sometimes a stress on the "and" of beat 2. Used frequently by pianist Bill Evans, e.g. the tunes "Alice in Wonderland" and "Some day my Prince will come".

key description of a piece or section of a piece in which the music adheres in general (there may be a number of chromatic notes) to the notes of a major or minor scale. A piece "in the key of" C major, e.g., will contain a melody using principally the notes of this major scale and chords derived from it.

kicks points of rhythmic emphasis in a given melody, often stressed by the accompanying left hand or bass and drums

Latin global term encompassing a number of rhythmic styles within jazz, combining improvisation with the rhythms of Latin America, including bossa nova, samba or salsa

lick short melodic or rhythmic phrase that becomes characteristic of a player's or group's style

major description of intervals (not 4ths, 5ths or octaves) where the gap between the two notes is the greater possible alternative: e.g. C to E in a major 3rd (cf. C–E♭, a minor 3rd). Description of a chord where the 3rd is major and of a scale where the succession of intervals is tone, tone, semitone, tone, tone, tone, semitone.

medium swing see swing (1)

middle eight see bridge

minor description of intervals (not 4ths, 5ths or octaves) where the gap between the two notes is the smaller possible alternative: e.g. C–E♭ in a minor 3rd (cf. C–E, a major 3rd). Description of a chord where the 3rd is minor and of two possible types of scale where the succession of intervals at the top varies but where in each case the 3rd is a minor 3rd.

mode type of scale with a distinct arrangement of tones and semitones. Examples are the Dorian, Mixolydian and Lydian modes.

modulation the movement within a piece or

section of a piece from one key to another

motive short musical idea—rhythmic, melodic or harmonic—used as the basis for development in improvisation

neighbor notes notes a step away from the note concerned in the scale. Chromatic notes are notes a semitone away.

New Orleans jazz early style of small-ensemble jazz originating in New Orleans in the 1910s and 1920s, from which many later styles, revivals and imitations (Dixieland, Traditional) emerged

open position type of voicing in which the notes of the chord are spaced for clarity

perfect description of the intervals of a 4th and 5th in their usual position: e.g. C–F (4th), C–G (5th)

polyrhythm superimposition of one rhythm or pulse upon another

pulse created by the division of time into regular beats at a particular speed

Rhythm and Blues (R'n'B) guitar-based blues style that grew up alongside jazz, continued the boogie-woogie tradition within jazz piano and led, in one offshoot, to rock-n-roll in the 1950s

rhythm section usually the piano, bass and drums, sometimes also with guitar and percussion. A group of instruments whose role is to define the groove and then vary it continually throughout a solo, creating a range of textures and dynamics in interaction with the soloist. They also provide a rhythmic and harmonic context for a solo and sometimes take on a more soloistic role themselves. In more popular styles the rhythm section tend to be more fixed in their roles, while in jazz they are given more flexibility.

rhythmic placement the ability to place a note, phrase or chord on a particular place in the measure

riff a repeated melodic phrase or bass-line. Often used in interaction with a given texture or with other riffs to create an exciting polyphonic texture or build-up behind a solo or melody.

rock (1) led from the bass-drum, a rock groove is usually in 4/4 and has a backbeat on beats 2 and 4, often on the snare drum in a band context
(2) global term for a number of styles of guitar-based popular music, which grew from rock-n-roll and first became popular in the 1950s and 1960s

root the bass note of a chord

samba Latin 2 feel groove, with an accent on beat 2. Felt at a walking pace, it was originally the music of carnival, but is now found at a range of tempos.

Scat singing vocal improvising, usually without words, or where words are made up that create good textures or appropriate attacks for the rhythmic character of the improvising

sequence see chord sequence

seventh chord chord formed from the root, 3rd, 5th and 7th degrees of a scale. Often voiced with 5th omitted.

slow swing see swing (1)

song form name given to the structure of a typical 32-measure standard: AABA. The B section is known as the middle eight or bridge.

straight ahead jazz sometimes also called mainstream. Grew out of bebop and the various jazz movements of the 1950s, and implies the conventional or straightforward jazz of bebop and its derivatives. Usually swing feel, and contrasted with the more eclectic approaches of Latin jazz, jazz-rock and free jazz.

straight 8s feel indication in which the beat is subdivided into two

stride style of jazz piano playing in which the left hand "strides" between bass notes or (rolled) 10ths on beats 1 and 3 of a 4/4 measure and chords around the middle of the keyboard on beats 2 and 4. Notable exponents were "Fats" Waller and Art Tatum.

substitution replacement of one or more chords of the standard blues sequence with others, to create a richer effect or provide more movement

swing (1) led from the ride cymbal, swing is a feel indication in which each beat is subdivided broadly into three —a triplet feel. Often seen at the start of a melody as slow swing, medium swing or up swing, indicating the tempo concerned. Common in jazz from the 1920s to the present.
(2) style of jazz that also became the popular music of the 1930s and 1940s, characterized by the big band sound and the triplet subdivision (see (1) above). Key players included Count Basie, Duke Ellington and on piano "Fats" Waller, Art Tatum and Erroll Garner. Also, in the more commercial form, Benny Goodman, Tommy

Dorsey and Glenn Miller.

syncopation   stressing notes other than the main beats of the measure

tendency tones   another name for guide tones

ten-to-ten   name for the characteristic swing rhythm played on the ride cymbal of a drum-kit. In 4/4 it is heard as:

Traditional jazz   see New Orleans jazz

triad   chord formed from the root, 3rd and 5th degrees of a scale

triad over bass note   style of harmony, where chords are created by choosing a bass note and a triad to go above it, which creates a particular modal context for improvising. Used particularly after 1950 as a way of widening the available palette of chords and voicings. Also a way of notating these chords, e.g. Bb/C = a triad of Bb over a C bass note. (see also chord symbol)

triad tones   tones 1, 3 and 5 of a given triad, often used to create the backbone of an improvisation over that triad

turnaround   chordal progression at the end of a section or solo and leading to the next section or back to the head. (I)–VI–II–V is a typical example.

twelve-bar blues   chord sequence lasting twelve measures which became popular and standardized in the early part of the century and has formed the basis of much popular music and jazz since then. Also implies a particular melodic vocabulary and a way of playing.

II–V–I   "two-five-one"; name of a common chord progression using the chords IIm7–V7–IΔ

upbeat   see downbeat

up swing   see swing (1)

vamp   repeated phrase, often containing a particular rhythmic, melodic and harmonic character or idea; useful to improvise over and often found in the introductions to tunes or as a holding device at particular points in jazz forms

voicings   The spacing, layout and combination of notes in a chord which helps produce the characteristic sonorities within different jazz styles

walking bass   often on the (plucked) string bass, a steady quarter note line at the bottom of a swing texture which defines a swing groove and creates the harmonic basis by stating and interacting with the roots, triad tones and other notes in the harmony

CD Track Listing

TRIO TAKES
1. Prove You Groove
2. Is You Is, or Is You Ain't (Ma' Baby)
3. He Is Sadly Melting

PIECES: BLUES
4. Introduction
5. Bedford Square Blues
6. O, Lord, Please Don't Let Them Drop That Atomic Bomb on Me
7. O, Lord, Please Don't Let Them Drop That Atomic Bomb on Me (embellished version)
8. Bags' Groove
9. Slinky Thing
10. Prove You Groove

PIECES: STANDARDS
11. Introduction
12. Perdido
13. Inchworm
14. Jean Pierre
15. (Old Man from) The Old Country
16. Is You Is, or Is You Ain't (Ma' Baby)

PIECES: CONTEMPORARY JAZZ
17. Introduction
18. Bottle Junction
19. Blue Autumn
20. He Is Sadly Melting
21. Here We Go Again
22. Yokate

PIECES: MINUS ONE TRACKS
23. Introduction
24. Bags' Groove
25. Perdido
26. Yokate

ROUTINES OF MINUS ONE TRACKS
Bags' Groove: 4 solos
Perdido: 8 solos
Yokate: 8 solos

AURAL TESTS
exam set
27. Introduction
28. Test A (book no. 1)
29. Test B (book no. 1)
30. Test C: sung response (book no. 1)
31. Test C: played response (book no. 1)

practice tests
32. Introduction
33. Test A1
34. Test A2
35. Test A3 (trio)
36. Test A4
37. Test A5 (trio)
38. Test A6
39. Test A7

QUICK STUDIES
40. Introduction
41. No. 11 by ear
42. No. 9 at sight

SCALES
43. Introduction
44. Dorian on D, right hand, straight
45. Mixolydian on G, left hand, swing
46. C major, right hand, swing
47. Major pentatonic on C, right hand, straight
48. ♭3 pentatonic on G, left hand, swing
49. G major arpeggio, left hand, straight
50. D minor arpeggio, right hand, swing

Presenter: Geoffrey Smith
Pianists: Charles Beale, Pete Churchill, Michael Garrick, Nikki Iles
Drums: Trevor Tomkins *Bass:* Tim Wells *Exam "candidates":* John Hayward, Nathan Hayward